Yorkshire Dales: **Walks to Viewpoints**

First published in 2023 by:

Northern Eye Books Limited

Northern Eye Books, Tattenhall, Cheshire CH3 9PX

© Northern Eye Books Limited 2023

ISBN 978-1-914589-17-1

Text: *Frank Kew*

Series editor: *Tony Bowerman*

Photographs: *Neil Bland, Neil Coates, Stephan Brzozowski, Adobe Stock, Alamy, Dreamstime, Shutterstock, Wikimedia Commons*

Design: *Carl Rogers and Laura Hodgkinson*

Frank Kew has asserted his rights under the Copyright, Designs and Patents Act, 1988 to be identified as the author of this work. All rights reserved.

A CIP catalogue record for this book is available from the British Library.

Printed in the EU by Latitude on woodland-friendly FSC stock

Cover: *Glacial erratic at Twisleton Scars (Walk 5)*

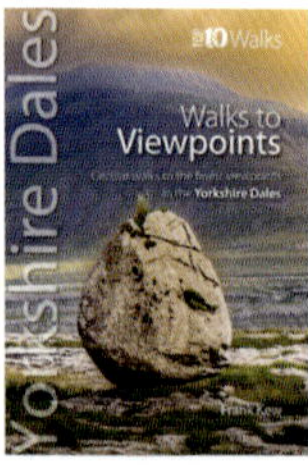

www.northerneyebooks.co.uk

@northerneyebooks

@northerneyeboo

@northerneyebooks

For sales enquiries, please call 01928 723 744

tony@northerneyebooks.co.uk

Contents

Kirby Stephen
A66
2
38
A685
Richmond
A683
A1
M6
Swaledale
A6108
37
Sedburgh
Hawes
Leyburn
A684
A684
A684
A683
A684
9
10
A6108
YORKSHIRE DALES
Kirkby
Lonsdale
NATIONAL PARK
A65
5
6
A687
Ingleton
8
1
A65
Patley
Bridge
Grassington
Settle
3
Malham
4
7
A682
SKIPTON
A59
A59
A629
A65
Ilkley

Pennine Perfection

Created in 1954, the **Yorkshire Dales National Park** covers 2,178 square kilometres/841 square miles of the central Pennines. As well as some of Yorkshire's most magnificent landscapes, the National Park also includes parts of historic Lancashire and Westmorland such as the Orton and Howgill Fells and the Lune Valley. Upwards of 8 million visitors a year enjoy this striking countryside with its picturesque stone villages.

The 'Dales' is something of a misnomer, for in addition to the beautiful dales, the area incorporates great tracts of wild moorland, the famous 'Three Peaks', and an intriguing industrial heritage. Over 1,300 miles of rights of way allow walkers to explore all aspects of the Park. In addition, almost 11,000 hectares of 'open access' land provides boundless possibilities for exploring this heady mix of limestone and gritstone scenery.

Taking in the view from Malham Cove

The Yorkshire Dales' finest views

Many memories of walks in the Dales are distilled into the fine views one experiences, and it would be a mistake to assume that great views necessarily entail sustained climbs to the top of the nearest fells. As Wordsworth would have it, one might be 'surprised by joy' when coming out of a belt of woodland into fields, or onto the edge of a limestone outcrop, or discovering a hidden valley.

Finding a contouring path with a panorama of the bucolic dale below slowly unfolding is so rewarding, as is contemplating the changes of light as the shadows of clouds play upon the wide open moorlands so characteristic of the Yorkshire Dales.

"The same view that I have seen a million times never fails to amaze me."

Alistair Brownlee, *local triathlete*

TOP **10 Walks:** Walks to Viewpoints

THESE WALKS REFLECT THE VARIETY OF SCENERY in the landscapes of the Yorkshire Dales. The underlying geology, mainly of gritstone and limestone, gives rise to different farming practices and other land use which, in turn, provide different vistas and experiences for the walker. Classic Dales' scenery of limestone pavements, scars and screes features strongly as do the atmospheric limestone gorges formed by glacial action. The two main upland glacial lakes in the Dales and their associated wetlands also feature, as do some lovely riverside strolls through flower-rich meadows. Enjoy!

Twisleton Scars
page 32

Upper Wharfedale
page 36

Flasby Fell
page 42

Capplestone Gate
page 48

Semerwater
page 54

Dentdale &
Deepdale
page 60

Moughton Scar at the head of Crummack Dale

Crummack Dale

Enjoy classic limestone scenery in a secluded valley with stunning views throughout

Distance/Time: 7 miles/11 kilometres. Allow 3½ – 4 hours
Start: The Game Cock Inn, Austwick LA2 8BB
Grid ref: SD 768 686
Ordnance Survey Map: Explorer OL2 Yorkshire Dales Southern & Western Areas *Whernside, Ingleborough & Pen-y-ghent*
After the Walk: The Game Cock Inn, The Green, Austwick, Nr. Settle LA2 8BB | 015242 51226 | info@gamecockinn.co.uk OR Elaine's Tearooms, Home Barn, Feizor, Lancaster LA2 8DF | 01729 824114 | e.knowles00@btinternet.com

Walk outline: The route ascends the south-eastern edge of the Ingleborough massif where the famous Norber Erratics, boulders deposited by retreating ice-sheets, are found. From here, the route follows limestone outcrops and scree to the head of Crummack Dale. Crossing the spectacular Moughton Scars, the return route descends to the valley bottom and across fields to pass the farm at Crummack. An ancient clapper bridge crosses Austwick Beck and onto a lovely green lane leading to the hamlet of Wharfe. From there, it is a short meander back to Austwick.

Crummack Dale

Crummack Dale, only 2.5 kilometres in length, is defined by an amphitheatre of limestone outcrops, lying between the upland massifs of Long Scar to the west and Moughton Scar to the east. Much of the dale is inaccessible by car and the network of tracks and green lanes is a walker's paradise. The route follows the edge of the dale with its unfolding panorama of limestone pavement and scars, and the looming bulks of Ingleborough and Pen-y-ghent in the distance. This is classic Dales' scenery at its best. Crummack Dale, lying parallel with the much larger Ribblesdale, is a hidden gem.

What to expect:
A steady climb to open fell, panoramic views, limestone pavement, quiet lanes

Natural glacial 'erratic'

Northern Brown Argus

The Walk

1. Facing the **Game Cock Inn**, turn right up main street, and turn left onto

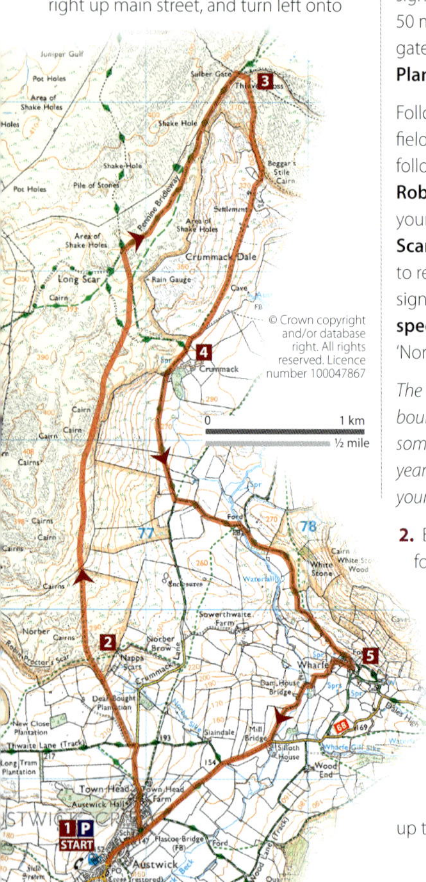

Townhead Lane. 300 metres past the last house, turn left onto **Thwaite Lane**, signposted 'Clapham and Norber'. 50 metres later, turn right through a gate into a field called '**Dear Bought Plantation**'.

Follow the track diagonally across the field. Do not go through the gate, but follow the wall to cross the stile below **Robin Proctor's Scar**. As the wall on your left bends to the left below the **Scar**, bear right uphill for 50 metres to reach a signpost. Turn left here, signposted 'Norber' and ascend to the **spectacular boulder field** known as the 'Norber Erratics'.

The Norber Erratics are silurian sandstone boulders deposited when glaciers retreated some 12,000 years ago. They are 430 million years old, and sit on top of the much younger limestone bedrock.

2. Bear right below a **large cairn** and follow the path between two large **sandstone 'erratics'.** Keep ahead, climbing gently, aiming for the wall corner and **ladder stile** about 200 metres ahead. Cross the stile and bear right following the path contouring between limestone screes, and generally parallel with the wall on the right. Do not follow routes climbing higher up the fell.

Descending from Sulber Gate

After 1 kilometre, the way passes above a **copse** next to Crummack Farm down in the valley. Do not descend, but keep ahead across a shallow valley, to a **broad track** parallel with the wall on your right. At a fork bear right onto the **Pennine Bridleway**.

Here, there are stunning views of Ingleborough to the west and Pen-y-ghent to the east – two of the celebrated 'Three Peaks' of the Dales, the other being Whernside.

Keep ahead and soon Moughton Scars, at the head of Crummack Dale, come into view down to the right. Some

1.5 kilometres from Crummack, the path arrives at **Sulber Gate**. Do not go through Sulber Gate, but turn right through a smaller gate in the wall.

The coloration of the much-degraded limestone pavement above Moughton Scar is made up of red and green whetstone and lies completely flat. Striations indicate the direction of flow of the overlying glacier.

3. Descend steeply to the limestone pavement. After 50 metres, bear right and generally southwards, on a path across the pavement waymarked by **two stone cairns**. This soon becomes a grassy

Limestone scars frame the head of Crummack Dale

path between limestone outcrops to reach **Beggar's Stile**, and the path to the valley bottom.

Just after Beggar's Stile, the path crosses the ruins of a large **D-shaped enclosure**. *This, and other enclosures and rectangular buildings to the left, are remnants of an early medieval farmstead.*

Continue down the dale southwards, aiming for a copse of trees at **Crummack farmstead**.

Crummack Farm first appears in the written record in the C12th as 'Crombok'. The name may be one of the few old British (ie. pre-Norse) place names in the Dales, deriving from 'crumbaco', meaning 'crooked hill'.

4. Follow the yellow waymarkers to reach a broad track. Continue for 700 metres, and turn left onto a green lane signposted 'Wharfe 1¼m'. Cross the **ancient clapper bridge** over **Austwick Beck**.

On the right is the historic Austwick Washdub. Farmers would dam the beck to create a pool or 'washdub' to 'salve' the sheep with grease and wash the fleeces to rid them of parasites, ready for market.

Continue to follow this walled lane as it winds down **Crummack Dale** and into the village of **Wharfe** at **Garth Cottage**.

5. Turn right passing a **row of houses**, and take the unmarked footpath to the left. This walled path follows **Austwick Beck** between fields to reach the main road at **Silloth House**.

This road was part of the C18th Keighley — Kendal turnpike route through Settle,

Austwick, Clapham, and Ingleton, before the A65 was built by-passing these villages.

Turn right into **Austwick** to complete the walk at the **Game Cock Inn**. ♦

'Dear Bought'?

Below the Norber Erratics is a field called 'Dear Bought Plantation'. In local legend, a farmer's son suggested to his father that he retire and make the farm over to his son. The father said he would do so but only if the son could single-handedly mow a particular field with a scythe in 24 hours. The son completed the task but collapsed and died. Since that day, the field has been known as 'dear bought'.

Extensive limestone pavement near Orton

Orton & Beacon Hill

An exhilarating walk to a limestone plateau with extensive views over Lunesdale and the Upper Eden valley

Distance/Time: 4 miles/6.5 kilometres. Allow 3 – 3½ hours

Start: Church of All Saints, Orton CA10 3RU

Grid ref: NY 622 085

Ordnance Survey Map: Explorer OL19 Howgill Fells and Upper Eden Valley

After the Walk: Orton Scar Café, Silver Yard, Orton CA10 3RQ | 015396 24421 OR The George Hotel, Front Street, Orton CA10 3RJ | 015396 24071 | www.thegeorgehotelorton.co.uk

Walk outline: A lovely green lane leads out of Orton into flower-rich meadows to climb gently onto the limestone pavement of Beacon Hill. Here, at the high point of this breathtaking walk, are outstanding long-distance views south to the Howgill Fells, west to the eastern fells of the Lake District, and north to Cross Fell. The return route sweeps round the western flank of Great Asby Scar to reach a Neolithic stone circle, before crossing fields to return into the picturesque village of Orton. Don't miss the famous chocolate shop!

Orton and Beacon Hill

The raised limestone plateaux of the Orton Fells are part of the recent north-westerly extension to the Yorkshire Dales National Park, even though the area, historically, is known as the Westmorland Dales. To the north of Orton, which Wainwright described as 'one of Westmorland's loveliest villages,' is a complex mix of limestone pavements at a height of around 350 metres, including Beacon Hill and the National Nature Reserve of Great Asby Scar. The area is famous for its wildflower meadows and species-rich roadside verges, yet remains relatively undiscovered by walkers.

Orton church

Autumn gentian

The Walk

1. Facing the porch of the **Church of All Saints**, turn right and walk down to cross the **Appleby Road**. Keep straight ahead on a minor road and, after 100 metres, turn left, due north, onto a bridleway signposted 'B6260 Orton Scar'. After 100 metres, and at the northern edge of the village, bear left onto a **green lane** signposted 'B6260'. On leaving the village, the track follows **Orton Beck** on the right, through flower meadows and up to **Broadfell Farm** about 1km from Orton.

Orton boasts some of the best upland hay meadows in the Dales best seen in spring and early summer. Look out for wood cranesbill, great burnet, and pignut. The village has benefited from the Coronation Meadows initiative which seeks to establish and extend flower meadows around the country.

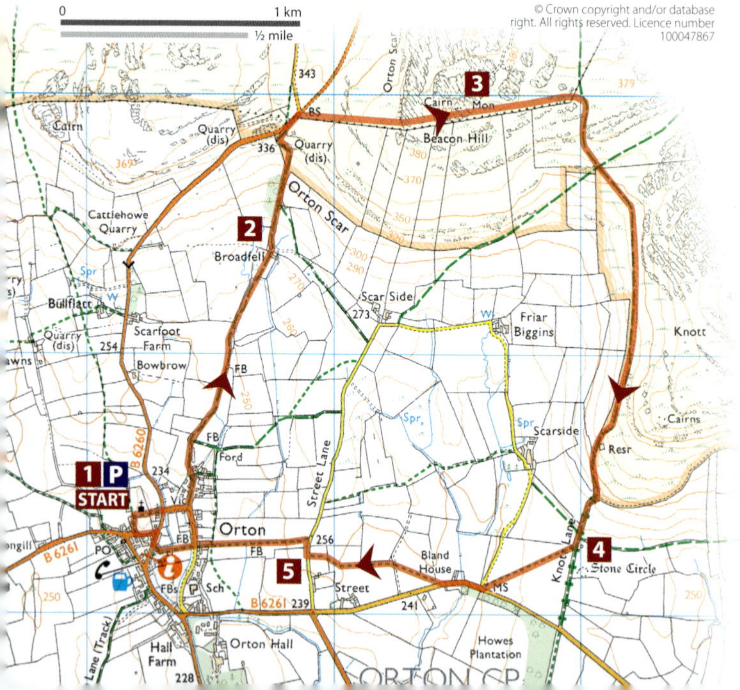

2. Bear left through the farmyard and the way steepens to climb **Orton Scar** to reach an **old quarry** and then the **B6260**, the Orton/Appleby road. Turn right up the road and, at the junction with the road to Crosby Ravensworth, turn right onto the fellside (at an old **Boundary Stone**). The path follows a wall on the right all the way to **Beacon Hill Monument**, about 500 metres east of the road.

Beacon Hill is on the Westmorland Plateau which separates the catchments of the River Lune and the River Eden. The monument was built by John Bland of nearby Reagill, to commemorate the Golden Jubilee of Queen Victoria in 1887 during the high summer of the British Empire. Standing at a height of 392 metres above sea level, it provides superb views over the Howgill range to the south, the Upper Eden valley to the north, and some of the peaks of the Eastern Lake District to the west. Great Asby Scar and Knott Hill are to the east. In the past, fires were lit at the beacon as a warning signal of approaching Scottish border raiders.

3. Continue eastwards on the path by the wall to a wall corner where the wall turns northwards. A hundred metres later, turn right through a gate and bear right downhill.

Clouds gather above Beacon Hill

At a path crossing, it is worth a **detour** here to visit the vast limestone pavement of **Great Asby Scar**. To do so, turn left at this path junction and walk uphill. Retrace your steps to this path crossing.

Keep ahead, downhill and generally southwards, to follow the contouring path which skirts the western flank of the **Great Asby Nature Reserve**. After about 1km from the top, the bridleway leaves the Nature Reserve through a gate and on to **Knott Lane**. After 200 metres, take the second path over a stile on the right.

But at this point, take another **detour** to visit **Gamelands Stone Circle** in the field on the right about 100 metres ahead. *The stones, set out in an oval shape, are mainly pink granite and have partially been robbed out. But around 33 of the original 40+ stones remain. It is one of the largest stone circles in Cumbria and dates from the late Neolithic period, around 2500BC.*

4. Return to the path junction. The way ahead is diagonally across the field in a south-westerly direction towards a **belt of woods**. Keep ahead onto the main road and turn right to pass **Bland House**. Fifty metres after the house turn right over a stile signposted 'Street Lane'. Cross the field diagonally to another stile and keep ahead to reach **Street Lane**, as the distinctive white church tower of Orton comes into view.

© Stephan Brzozowski

All Saints Church dates from the C12th; the tower was built in the early C16th, and the porch is dated 1607. In 2006, the tower was rendered in lime, giving it its distinctive white appearance.

5. Turn right on Street Lane and, after 50 metres, turn left signposted 'Orton'. The path crosses a **stream** and enters **Orton village** by way of a narrow **walled path** to complete the walk. ♦

The Orton Dobbie

'Dobbie' is Westmorland vernacular for 'a mischievous spirit'. The Orton Dobbie is thought to be the ghost of a man who was murdered on his way home from Kendal. It's said that in a house in Orton during the C19th, a child's cradle was overturned and furniture was seen to move around the floor, an event blamed locally on 'the Orton Dobbie.' Experts in the paranormal have tried but never solved the spooky mystery.

Walkers enjoying the views from Malham Cove

Malham & Watlowes

An exhilarating walk with fine views over Malham Tarn and Malham Cove

Distance/Time: 6 miles/9 kilometres. Allow 3½ – 4 hours

Start: YDNP Information Centre Carpark, Malham BD23 4DA

Grid Ref: SD 901 628

Ordnance Survey Map: Explorer OL2, Yorkshire Dales Southern & Western areas, *Whernside, Ingleborough, & Pen-y-ghent*

After the Walk: The Old Barn, Chapel Gate, Malham, Skipton BD23 4DA 01729 830486 | theoldbarnmalham@gmail.com OR The Buck Inn, Cove Road, Malham, Skipton, BD23 4DA 01729 830317 | buckinn.malham@stonegategroup.co.uk

Walk outline: Whilst most walkers make a bee-line for Malham Cove, this route strikes westwards to reach the high ground of Kirkby Fell and Ewe Moor 'far from the madding crowd'. There are spectacular views of the glacial lake and the complex of limestone pavement which makes up the Malham Tarn Estate. It is an easy stroll across fields to the head of the dry limestone valley of Watlowes. This leads to the limestone pavement above Malham Cove with superb views southwards down Malhamdale. A route across ancient village fields, again off the beaten track, reaches the village and well-earned refreshments.

Climbers, Malham Cove

Malham

Originally an Anglian settlement from the C7th and C8th, most of today's village houses date from the C18th. Just north of the village is Malham Cove – how spectacular must have been the waterfall sweeping over the Cove at the end of the last Ice Age. Just north of the Cove is the Malham Tarn Estate, a National Trust property containing some of the most dramatic upland limestone landscape in the country. The Tarn and surrounding wetlands became a National Nature Reserve in 1992.

Peregrine pair

The Walk

1. From the **YDNP car park**, walk back to the road and take the **walled track** to the side of the carpark signposted 'Pike Daw'. After 50 metres bear right as the track runs northwards parallel with the village **Main Street**. At the first junction, just before the track re-enters the village, turn left uphill on a broad stony track which soon swings right.

Just after **Burns Barn**, and the **water treatment plant**, turn left at a fork in the track. The track links up several **field barns** and then bears left to cross a **beck**.

2. Turn right, over a wall stile and head across the field to the right of **Butterlands Barn**. Keep ahead as the path ascends the field with a beck on the left, and onto open fell between Kirkby Fell (546m/1791ft) on the left and Pikedaw Hill (460m/1509ft) to the right. As the ground levels out, keep ahead, generally westwards, aiming for the field gate in the wall ahead with a **cairn** beyond. This is the highest point on the walk at 490m/1608ft.

3. Turn right on a broad track which is part of the **Dales High Way**. Look out for **Nappa Cross** on the wall on the right.

Nappa Cross is a medieval way-marker which, although incongruously built into a wall, would have stood originally at the junction of two nearby packhorse tracks across Malham Moor, much of which was owned and farmed by Fountains Abbey until the Dissolution of the monasteries in 1539. From here, there are superb views over Malham Tarn owned by the National Trust. The Tarn is one of only eight upland alkaline lakes in Europe and has been designated as a Special Site of Scientific Interest.

Keep ahead across four fields, gradually descending to a T-junction with

The Pennine Bridleway. Turn right, signposted Langscar Gate. At **Langscar Gate**, cross the road and keep ahead to the bottom of the field. Cross the **ladder stile** on the left signposted Watlowes.

4. Turn right and descend the steps to the bottom of **Watlowes**.

This deep limestone canyon was formed by glacial overspill which would have fed a waterfall over the mighty Malham Cove. Today it is a dry valley as rainwater percolates through cracks and gullies in the limestone to re-appear as a stream at the foot of the cove. However, during Storm

Malham Tarn – a rare upland alkaline lake

Desmond in December 2015, the resulting deluge filled up the system, and surface water flowed down Watlowes and over the Cove making, for a brief couple of hours, Britain's highest waterfall.

Continue down Watlowes and, leaving the National Trust's **Malham Tarn Estate**, reach the **limestone pavement** at the top of **Malham Cove**.

Limestone pavements are formed by the scouring action of ice sheets exposed when the glaciers retreated. Typically, they comprise of 'clints' and 'grykes'. Clints are the flat horizontal slabs of limestone, whilst grykes are the deep vertical cracks and fissures, formed by the action of rainwater exploiting lines of weakness in the rocks. A scene from Harry Potter and the Deadly Hallows was filmed here.

Turn right to cross the limestone pavement (slippy when wet), at the end of which is the stepped path down to the bottom of the cove. At the end of the stone steps, take the left fork to visit the cove bottom.

This is the headwater of Malham Beck. South of the village is 'Aire Head' — the headwater of the River Aire, which flows through Skipton and Leeds on it's way to the North Sea.

5. Take the broad path southwards towards Malham but, after 200 metres, cross the **stone bridge** over the beck, and bear right up the hill through some ancient fields.

These fields, with their strip lynchets and terraces, bear testimony to the foundation of the village by Anglo-Saxons in the C7th. Barley and oats would have been grown.

The path enters the **village** near **The Listers Arms**. Turn right down the road to reach the YDNP car park. ♦

Malham's lost chapel
The remains of the long-lost St Helen's Chapel have been found in the field to the south-west of the YDNP car park. Built in the C12th, it was a chapel-of-ease for parishioners who could not access the parish church in Kirkby Malham. Most land around Malham was owned by Fountains Abbey and Bolton Priory. This was surrendered to the Crown at the time of the Dissolution of the monasteries by Henry VIII, and the chapel was demolished in 1549.

Negotiating the boulder-strewn entry to Trollers Gill

Trollers Gill & Appletreewick

A walk of contrasts from an atmospheric gorge, to views over Wharfedale and a bucolic riverside stroll

What to expect:
Rocky gorge, open fell with superb views, and riverside walking

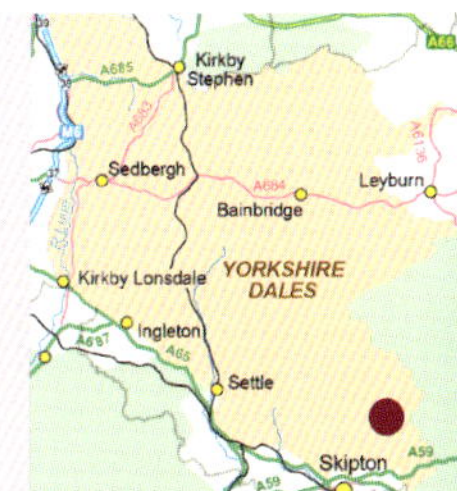

Distance/Time: 6½ miles/10.5 kilometres. Allow 3½ – 4 hours

Start: Parcevall Hall, Skyreholme BD23 6DE

Grid ref: SE 069 612

Ordnance Survey Map: Explorer OL2 Yorkshire Dales Southern & Western areas *Whernside, Ingleborough & Pen-y-ghent*

After the Walk: Parcevall Hall Tearooms, Skyreholme, Skipton BD23 6DE | 01756 720630 | www.parcevallhall.org.uk OR The Craven Arms, Appletreewick, Skipton BD23 6DA | 01756 720270

Walk outline: The walk begins with a stroll alongside a delightful beck before entering the atmospheric limestone gorge of Trollers Gill. At the top of the gorge, the way ahead, over rough pasture and moorland, provides superb views over Wharfedale with Barden Moor beyond. Descending to the picturesque village of Appletreewick and the valley bottom, the route continues along the riverbank passing some pretty waterfalls, before a climb to an ancient trackway on the flank of the imposing fell of Simon's Seat. There are lovely views over Parcevall Hall and the hamlet of Skyreholme before crossing fields to complete this walk of contrasts.

Craven Arms' real fire

Trollers Gill and Appletreewick

Trollers Gill was formed by glacial meltwater at the end of the last Ice Age. It has attracted a number of myths and legends: beware the 'trolls' who have a nasty habit of rolling stones down onto unsuspecting travellers in the gorge below. Appletreewick, or 'Aptrick' for locals, is an ancient settlement mentioned in the Domesday Book, and was a centre for lead mining until the C19th. Sir William Craven, a son of the village, became Lord Mayor of London in 1610.

Bloody cranesbill

The narrow chasm of Trollers Gill

The Walk

1. Just before the road **bridge** into **Parcevall Hall**, turn left into fields signposted 'New Road, 1 mile'. *The Parcevall Hall Estate was bought by Sir William Milner in 1927. He established the gardens, which contain trees and shrubs from China and Tibet. The Hall is now an official retreat for Bradford Diocese.*

The path up the valley follows **Skyreholme Beck** and skirts a **disused dam**. After some 750 metres, the path forks in front of the imposing **Middle Hill**. Bear right here, keeping parallel with the beck, to enter **Trollers Gill**.

Trollers Gill was formed by erosive activity from glacial meltwater over thousands of years. The top part was once a cave which has now collapsed. Legend has it that trolls lived here – a legend probably influenced by Norse settlement in the Dales.

Trollers Gill is generally dry, providing an enjoyable scramble through this atmospheric gorge for about ½ mile. Look out for an old **mine shaft**, or 'adit', high up on the right as you ascend.

2. The gill levels out and, 50 metres after the second **ladder stile**, cross the **beck** by a **wooden bridge** and pass through a gate to climb out of the valley. The wide, grassy path soon descends to meet a stony track. Keep ahead gradually climbing and in 50 metres, bear left off the track up a grassy slope, passing a huge **swallowhole** called 'Hell Hole' on the right. Keep ahead on a stone-flagged path to meet a minor road. Turn left for 50 metres to a sharp left-hand bend. Keep on the road and 100 metres after the bend, turn right through a gate signposted 'Hartlington 1¼ miles'.

3. You now enter **Appletreewick Pasture**. Keep ahead, gently descending, as superb views unfold over Wharfedale with Barden Moor beyond. After 1 kilometre, the track swings right through a gate onto a **walled track**. After 50 metres, turn left through a field gate signposted 'Appletreewick ¾ mile'. Follow this broad track downhill which swings left and then right, and becomes very steep and stony before

entering **Appletreewick** next to **The Craven Arms**.

The homely Craven Arms is named after Sir William Craven, Lord Mayor of London. A recent addition to the pub is a traditional 'cruck barn' – the first to be built in the Dales for over 300 years.

4. Facing the Craven Arms turn left, westwards, down the road for 200 metres

Middle Hill conceals the entry to Trollers Gill

and, just before a **campsite**, take the walled path on the left signed 'Riverside'.

At the **River Wharfe**, turn left downstream, signposted 'Barden Bridge', and follow the **riverside path** (part of the **Dales Way**), for about 1 kilometre to enter woodland passing beautiful **cascades**. The path bears away from the river to meet a road in the hamlet of **Howgill**. Cross the **bridge** and turn left signposted 'Howgill Lane ¼ mile'. Continue uphill to a path junction with Howgill Lane.

Howgill Lane was originally part of the old packhorse route between the markets of Skipton and Pateley Bridge. Look out for an old milestone on the right. This lane, on the lower flank of the imposing Simon's Seat, affords superb views over Wharfedale with Barden Moor beyond. The name of Simon's Seat is intriguing. One local legend is that Simon's Seat was named after an infant found here by a shepherd in the C19th. Another, is that it was named after Simon Magus, also known as Simon the Sorcerer, a shadowy religious figure from the C1st AD.

5. Turn left onto **Howgill Lane** and keep ahead for 1 kilometre where the track swings right and then left passing the farm buildings of **Eastwood Head**. Continue on the track for another 200 metres before turning left through a field gate signposted 'High Skyreholme'.

Follow the yellow waymarkers across fields to the **bridge** over **Blands Beck** and then uphill to reach the hamlet of **High Skyreholme**.

Skyreholme, from the Old Norse 'bright water meadow', had a cotton and calico mill in the C19th, supporting a village population of 234 in 1841.

6. Turn left downhill and follow the lane to cross a **bridge** and take the right-hand fork to reach **Parcevall Hall** to complete the walk. ♦

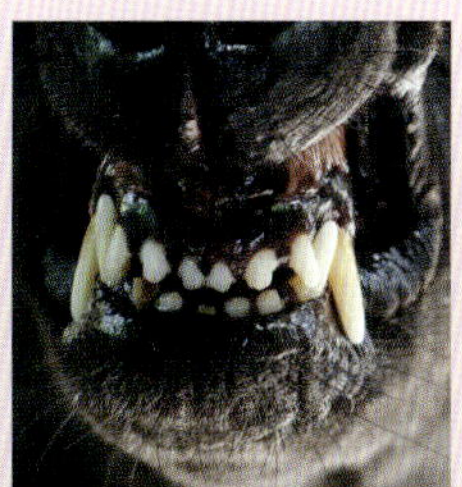

The Barghest of Trollers Gill

In folklore, the 'barghest' is a fearsome and monstrous black dog. The merest glance from his gimlet eyes can turn you to stone. 'The Legend of the Troller's Gill' (1830) recounts the tale of a man who ventures forth 'to the horrid gill of the limestone hill'…only for his body to be discovered with 'inhuman marks upon his breast.' This legend influenced Sir Arthur Conan Doyle in his 'Hound of the Baskervilles'!

Glacial erratic with Ingleborough beyond

Twisleton Scars

A circumnavigation of this limestone plateau provides stunning views of Ingleborough and beyond

Distance/Time: 6 miles/9.5 kilometres. Allow 3 – 3½ hours

Start: St Leonards Church Carpark, Chapel-le-Dale LA6 3AR

Grid ref: SD 739 771

Ordnance Survey Map: Explorer OL2, Yorkshire Dales Southern & Western Areas *Whernside, Ingleborough, and Pen-y-ghent*

After the Walk: Station Inn, Low Sleights Road, Ribblehead LA6 3AS | 015242 41274 | bookings@thestationinnribblehead.com OR White Scar Cave Café, Ingleton, LA6 3AW | 015242 41244 | info@whitescarcave.co.uk

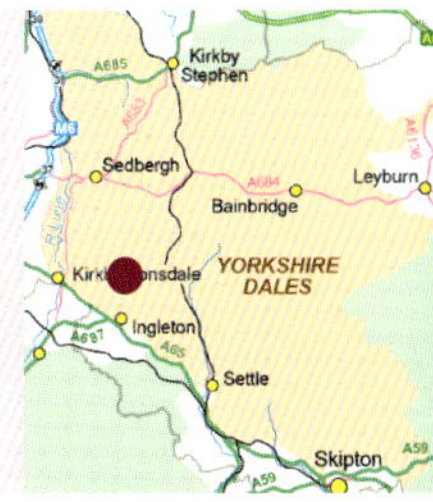

Walk outline: Start at the hamlet of Chapel-le-Dale with a gentle climb up through woods onto the open fell of Four Stones Rigg. Continue across peaty moorland passing many shakeholes to meet the extensive limestone pavement which caps Twisleton Scars. On reaching Scars End, the return route follows the scars edge with a grand panoramic view up the dale and over the looming bulk of Ingleborough. A return through woodland to the charming chapel of St Leonards completes the circuit.

The Twisleton Scars

This superb area of classic limestone scenery is the southern spur of the Whernside massif, separating Kingsdale Beck to the west from the River Doe to the east. The limestone pavement was formed when a glacier retreated some 15,000 years ago. Scattered across the limestone bedrock are big boulders of gritstone which have been deposited by the retreating ice. Since then, erosion to the sides of the plateau have created the complex of scars we see today. Twisleton Scars is the perfect place to view two of the famous 'Three Peaks' of the Dales – Whernside (736 metres) and Ingleborough (724 metres), as well as the equally famous Ingleborough Viaduct.

Twisleton Scars cairn

Wheatear

The Walk

1. Passing **St Leonards Church**, take the road on the right uphill and, after 70 metres, pass the impressive **Hurtle Pot** on the right.

Hurtle Pot is a flooded pothole famed for the 'glutting' sound of water in the cavern after heavy rains, which legend attributes to the 'Hurtlepot Boggart' lurking below.

Where the road swings left, keep ahead signposted 'Ellerbeck 1m'. Passing **Gill Head**, the track soon enters the Access Land of **High Scales Rigg** with scattered **limestone outcrops** and views of Whernside (736m) beyond. 500m later, there is a **ford** over **Ellerbeck Gill** at a T-junction.

2. Turn left, south-westwards, signposted 'Scars End 3.4m'. The way ahead is generally level, and after some 2km, the peaty path reaches outcrops of **limestone pavement**.

The path passes many 'shake holes', chock full of boulders and some 'pot holes'. Both are formed by rainwater, having collected on the overlying peat, finding it's way down through the porous limestone.

Keep ahead and, although the path becomes braided, aim for the **prominent boulder** ahead on the skyline. Fifty metres beyond this boulder, the path becomes wider and more well-defined. Soon, the way ahead is indicated by **blue marker posts**. The path continues to the right of **Ewes Top**, cuts through a limestone outcrop, and starts to descend to **Scars End**.

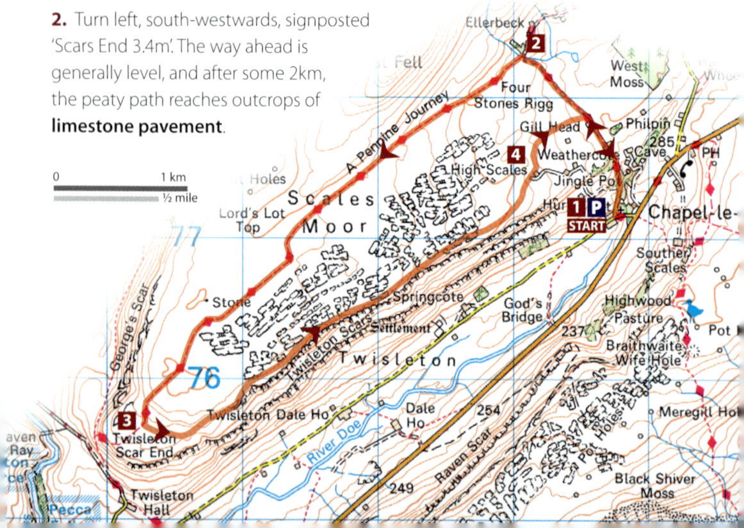

Cloud drapes over Ingleborough's summit

3. At this point turn left on the narrow path below a **limestone outcrop** and a **large cairn**. The way continues below the limestone outcrop meeting a wall on the right, and becomes well-defined in a north-easterly direction following the wall on the edge of **Twisleton Scars**.

Keep ahead for about 3 kilometres passing several cairns on the left. Do not attempt to descend the scar where the contouring wall disappears. The first habitation at the end of the scars is **High Scales** over the wall on the right.

4. Continue for a further 500 metres, following the field walls to reach a broad track at a field gate. Turn right downhill and retrace your steps back to Chapel-le-Dale to complete the walk. ◆

St Leonard's Church

This Grade II-listed church was used for the burials of navvies and their family members who died from accidents or disease whilst constructing Ingleborough Viaduct between 1869 and 1876. The graveyard had to be extended to accommodate them. Over two hundred people, including children, are listed in the Burial Register. A plaque in the church, memorialising the dead, was paid for by the Midland Railway Company.

A typical Dales' farmhouse in Langstrothdale

Upper Wharfedale

Enjoy memorable south-facing views from the head of Wharfedale

Distance/Time: 7 miles/11 kilometres. Allow 4 – 4½ hours

Start: YDNP car park (charges), Buckden BD23 5JX

Grid ref: SD 942 773

Ordnance Survey Map: Explorer OL 30, Yorkshire Dales, Northern & Central Areas, *Wensleydale & Swaledale*

After the Walk: Buck Inn, Buckden, Skipton BD23 5JX|01756 761933 | info@thebuckinn-buckden.co.uk OR West Winds Tearooms Buckden Skipton BD23 5JA|01756 760883

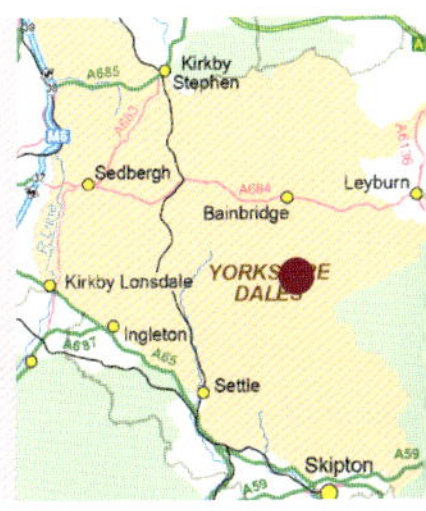

Walk outline: Riverside walking along the Dales Way is the main fare for the first part of this walk, firstly to the little village of Hubberholme, beloved of J.B.Priestley, and then onwards to the hamlet of Yockenthwaite in Langstrothdale. A short climb takes you up to a limestone escarpment which is the terminal feature of Wharfedale. Feast your eyes on the superb south-facing views down Wharfedale as the route unfolds towards the hamlet of Cray, before the final gradual descent to Buckden, again with lovely long-distance views.

Upper Wharfedale

The Upper Wharfedale Estate is owned and managed by The National Trust and contains many Sites of Special Scientific Interest and Special Areas of Conservation. It is one of the best places to see calcareous grasslands with ancient semi-natural woodlands on the valley sides, and flower-rich hay meadows on the valley bottom, dotted with barns once used for storing hay and over-wintering cattle. This is a classic U-shaped valley formed by glacial action and delineated by limestone sills and pavements above which are moorland habitats and blanket bog typical of the Dales.

National Trust 'omega' sign

Bee orchid

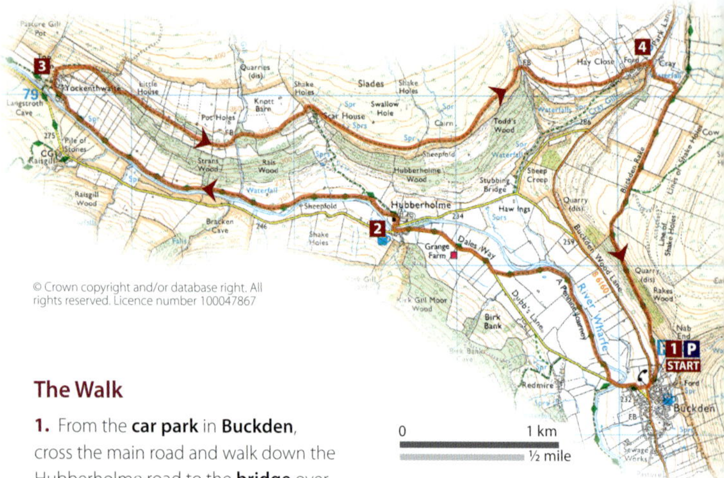

The Walk

1. From the **car park** in **Buckden**, cross the main road and walk down the Hubberholme road to the **bridge** over the infant **River Wharfe** .

This is called Election Bridge because its repair was promised in the manifesto of a prospective MP in the C18th.

Just after the bridge turn right onto the **Dales Way** signposted 'Hubberholme'. The path follows the west bank of the river for some 750 metres before leaving the river bank and crossing a field to a lane. Turn right and follow the lane into the hamlet of **Hubberholme** to arrive at **The George Inn** on the left.

The George, formerly the vicarage, maintains a tradition of lighting a candle on the bar. Auctions of agricultural land and grazing rights were held here, the last bid before the candle was extinguished being declared the winner.

2. Turn right over the bridge to arrive at the church of **St Michael and All Angels**.

Originally the 'forest chapel' of St Oswald in the Norman hunting forest of Langstrothdale Chase, it was built in the C12th on the site of a possible Anglo-Norse cemetery. The church is notable for its rood screen (dated 1558) which has a rood loft

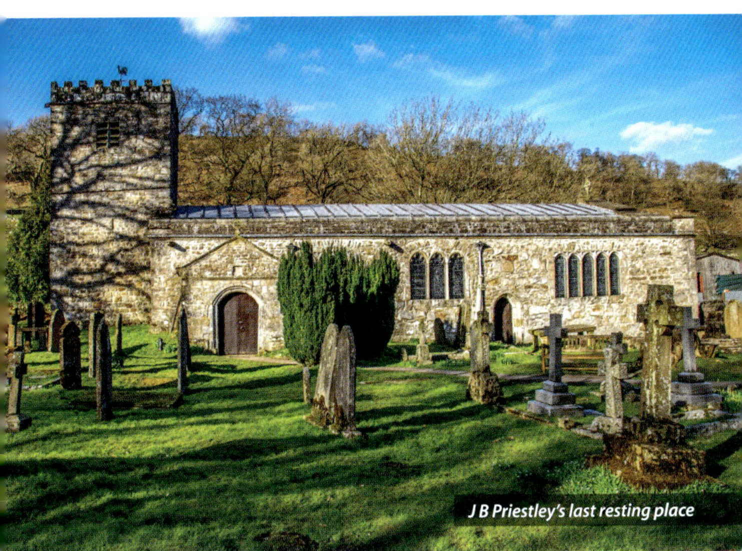

for musicians, one of only two surviving in Yorkshire. The ashes of J B Priestley were deposited in the graveyard and there is a plaque in the church. Priestley, who grew up in Bradford, called this 'the smallest, pleasantest place in the world'. The pews were crafted by the celebrated 'Mouse Thompson' in 1930. Look out for his trademark mice in the woodwork.

Walk past the church and take the footpath on the left by a **farm** signposted 'Dales Way and Yockenthwaite'. Leaving Wharfedale and entering **Langstrothdale**, the path follows the north bank of the **beck** for some 2 kilometres to reach the hamlet of **Yockenthwaite**.

Top Farm at Yockenthwaite was used in the most recent TV adaptation of 'All Creatures Great and Small'.

3. At Yockenthwaite, take the path uphill to the left of the **farmhouse** onto **moorland**. The path bears right, with a field wall on the right, to re-enter fields above **Strans Wood**. The route continues generally in an eastern direction on a contouring path for some 3.5 kilometres with fine views over, firstly

Dusk falls on Upper Wharfedale

Langstrothdale, and then the upper reaches of Wharfedale.

The view down Wharfedale is considered to be one of the finest in the Dales. This upper part of the dale forms an almost perfect U-shaped valley, formed by south-flowing glaciers during the last Ice Age which retreated around 12,000 years ago. The only habitation you will pass is the C18th Scar House which was the first land in the Dales owned by the Quakers and contains a Quaker burial ground.

About 1 kilometre after **Scar House**, you will pass **Cray Barrow** on the hill above you. *This is an early Bronze Age burial mound, containing the ashes or bones of a local person or family group, and located in a highly visible position on the skyline for those living and working in the fields below.*

4. On arrival at the hamlet of **Cray**, on the right is the C17th **White Lion Inn**, the highest pub in Wharfedale and formerly a drovers' inn.

Cray is on the route taken by the Tour de France in 2014 as the riders left Wharfedale and climbed Kidstones Pass en route for Bishopdale and beyond. An annual fell race from Cray to Buckden Pike and back is also held here.

Cross the road and take the **stepping stones** over cascading **Cray Gill**. Turn right and follow the signs uphill for some 200 metres. Turn right onto **Buckden Rake** which gradually descends to the car park in **Buckden**.

The final part of this walk follows the Roman Road between the forts at Ilkley *(Olicana)* in mid- Wharfedale and Bainbridge *(Virosidum)* in Wensleydale.

 West Winds Tearoom is situated behind **The Buck Inn**. ♦

Langstrothdale

Langstrothdale was first colonised by Anglians in the C7th but remained largely wooded through Norman times when it became a hunting forest governed by 'Forest Law'. But when the Earl of Clifford of Skipton Castle sold the land in 1604, dales folk could at last expand and consolidate their land holdings. The road through this remote dale was originally part of the packhorse route between Lancaster and Newcastle.

Summit of Sharp Haw – nearly there

Flasby Fell

Bag the two main peaks of Flasby Fell whilst enjoying views over Airedale and Barden Moor

Distance/Time: 7 miles/11.5 kilometres. Allow 4 – 4 ½ hours

Start: The Craven Heifer BD23 3LA

Grid ref: SD 983 534

Ordnance Survey Map: OL2 Explorer Yorkshire Dales Southern & Western Areas *Whernside, Ingleborough & Pen-y-ghent*

After the Walk: The Craven Heifer, Grassington Road, Town Moor, Skipton BD23 3LA |01756 792521 OR Cracoe Café, Ramskill Road, Cracoe, BD23 6LA | 01756 730228

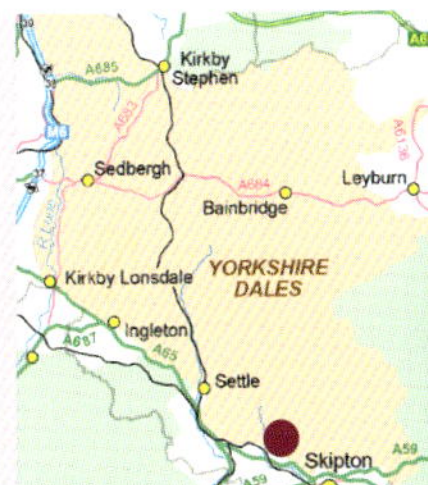

Walk outline: A gentle start across farmland before a steady climb up the conical-shaped slopes of Sharp Haw is rewarded by fine views. The way ahead to Rough Haw is clear from here. There follows a gentle descent across moorland and fields to the tiny hamlet of Flasby. The return route provides some contrasts with a stroll through lovely parkland before climbing through mixed woodland to open fell with great views over Airedale with Pendle Hill beyond. The final section retraces your steps to the Craven Heifer and a well-earned drink!

Sharp Haw 'trig point'

Flasby Fell

The distinctive hills of Sharp Haw and Rough Haw are the highest of the four summits which comprise Flasby Fell, an outlier of millstone grit upland on the south-western edge of the National Park; and they provide great views over the upper reaches of the Aire valley. Clearly visible from the main road up-dale from Skipton, they were dubbed 'the twin portals to the Yorkshire Dales'. Appropriately, the name 'haw' for these two hills derives from the Old English 'hawian', meaning 'view'.

Harebells

The Walk

1. From the **Craven Heifer**, turn right on the busy **B6265** for 100m and take the footpath on the left signposted 'Stirton'. Cross two fields to arrive at **Bog Lane**. Turn right and follow the lane round to the right and then to the left. At the third corner, keep ahead through a gate, signposted 'Flasby', and onto a broad track with a boundary wall on the left.

2. After two field gates, the route leaves the track and bears right, roughly north-westwards, across the fellside. Follow the obvious path, gently climbing, aiming for the conical hill ahead, ignoring a signpost pointing to the right. Cross the metal wall stile to gain the **trig point** on the **summit of Sharp Haw**.

Although only 1171ft/357m in height, there are superb views in every direction... Pendle Hill far to the SW, Rylstone Cross and Cracoe War Memorial on the western edge of Barden Moor to the NE, and Crookrise Crag to the east with Embsay Crag behind. Crookrise, a significant and historic gritstone edge for climbers, has been bought recently by the British Mountaineering Council.

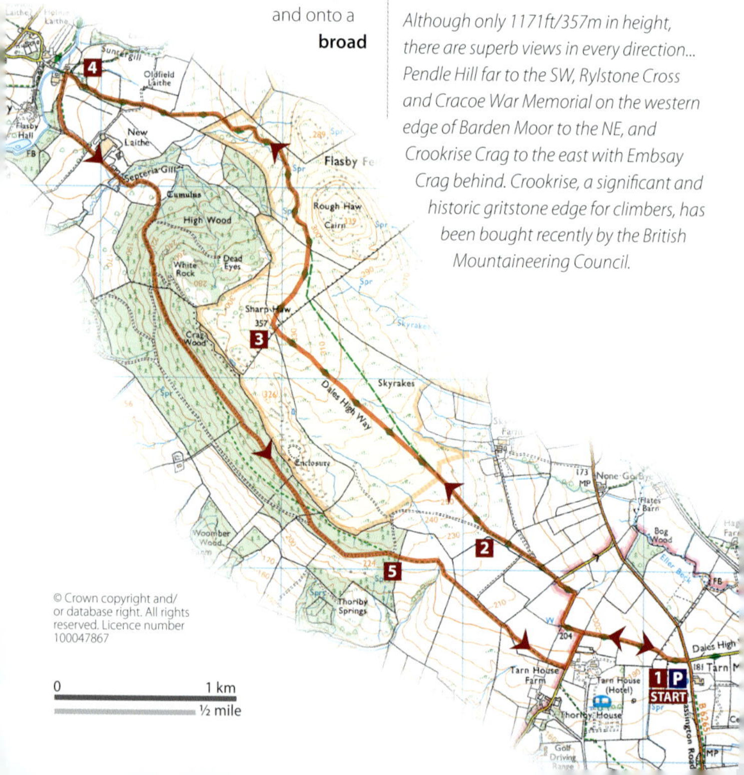

0   1 km

½ mile

Early morning cloud inversion from Sharp Haw

3. From the summit, bear right, north-eastwards, and descend on a path through a gap in the wall. The way ahead is downhill, for some 400 metres, then through a walkers' gate, before a short climb up to the **cairn** on **Rough Haw** (339 metres).

In prehistoric times, a stone rampart was built on Rough Haw following the contours along the steep scarp, and enclosing the summit. A break on the west side may have been the original entrance. The site is not defensible, so the enclosure may have had some ritual purpose in the Neolithic or the Bronze Age.

Retrace your steps to the walkers' gate and turn right, initially northwards, and follow the footpath downhill to the right of **High Wood** — boggy in places due to the number of springs, but persevere. Leaving the moor, the path crosses one field and onto a **broad track** which becomes an **ancient holloway** into the hamlet of **Flasby**.

Flasby, an old Norse settlement, is mentioned in the Domesday Book. An Iron Age sword and scabbard dating from the C1st AD, were found in the grounds of Flasby Hall. It is thought to have belonged to a warrior of the Brigantes, a

Rough Haw with Barden Moor beyond

Pennine tribe frequently in conflict with the Romans. Fred Truman, the famous Yorkshire and England cricketer, had his family home in Flasby, when he ran a sports shop in Skipton.

4. Turn left, onto a tarmac lane signposted 'Stirton 3 miles'. The lane swings left, uphill, passing **New Laithe Farm** on the left. Keep ahead through a gate into a large field. The broad track swings left and then right into **High Wood** via a kissing-gate. In the wood, the path climbs steadily and, at a steel bench, take the narrow path on the right. Bear left at a fork to leave the wood and reach a broad track. Bear left uphill and continue on this track for some 2 kilometres.

Along this track, there are good views over Airedale, the village of Gargrave, and the Leeds/Liverpool Canal. To the southeast of Gargrave, a Roman villa was built on the fertile land near the River Aire on the site of an earlier Brigantes settlement. Archaeologists have found mosaic floors, underfloor heating and a detached bathhouse which testify to its high status.

5. After some 2 kilometres, the track passes a **green shed** on the right. A hundred metres later and as the track swings sharp left, leave the track and follow a small path straight ahead to a wall stile and into a field. Cross this field, navigating a steep-sided **beck**. The path continues along a wall line on the left and then a fence line on the right to reach **Bog Lane**.

Turn left uphill passing **Tarn House Farm** and at the first left-hand bend in the road, turn right into fields to retrace your steps to the **B6265** and then to the pub, **The Craven Heifer,** to complete the walk. ♦

The 'Craven Heifer'

The original 'Craven Heifer' was bred by Rev William Carr of Bolton Abbey in 1807. To this day, she remains the largest cow ever shown in England, weighing 312 stone (1,132 kg) – so large that a special shed door twice as wide as the norm had to be built to house her. She only lived for five years, probably due to over-eating. Several pubs in the Craven district are named after her. This portrait in oils dates from 1811.

The winding entrance to Conistone Dib

Capplestone Gate

Panoramic views over Wharfedale unfold after reaching the top of a limestone gorge

Distance/Time: 6 miles/9.5 kilometres. Allow 4 – 4 ½ hours

Start: Conistone Bridge BD23 5HS (roadside parking)

Grid ref: SD 981 674

Ordnance Survey Map: Explorer OL2 Yorkshire Dales Southern and Western Areas *Whernside, Ingleborough & Pen-y-ghent*

After the Walk: The Tennant Arms Hotel, Mastiles Lane, Kilnsey, Skipton BD23 5PS | 01756 753946 OR The Café by the Lake, Kilnsey Park Estate, Skipton BD23 5PS | 01756 752150

Walk outline: The route up the spectacular glacial outflow of Conistone Dib gives way to fields and open moorland. In the footsteps of countless miners and drovers, it is a steady but undemanding climb up to the trig point at Capplestone Gate, the highest point of the walk at 1680ft/512m. The path winds between old mine workings before descending towards woodland and the Dales Way. The return route below limestone screes goes past the instantly recognisable Conistone Pie, before a short descent into Conistone village.

Capplestone Gate and Conistone Pie

The route up to the limestone outcrop of Capplestone Gate is on a medieval packhorse route over Conistone Moor with Nidderdale and Fountains Abbey beyond. Until the C19th, lead miners would also have passed this way en route for the workings nearby. The views over the looming bulk of Great Whernside to the north and Littondale to the west are superb. Coniston Pie, so named because its shape resembles a pork pie, is a limestone knoll just above Hill Castles Scar, affording great views over the ancient hamlet of Kilnsey and the iconic overhang of Kilnsey Crag.

Conistone Dib

Dropwort

The Walk

1. From the **crossroads** in the centre of **Conistone**, take the broad track eastwards and through a gate signposted 'Conistone Dib'. After a clamber over **limestone sills**, the narrow rock-strewn **Gurling Trough** provides the entrance to **Conistone Dib**.

This steep-sided gorge is dry except iafter prolonged winter rain. It was formed some 10 – 12,000 years ago by glacial meltwater pouring into the valley bottom as the glaciers retreated at the end of the last Ice Age.

Continue up Conistone Dib for some 1.25 kilometres as it widens out. It is a short scramble to climb out of the valley to meet the **Dales Way**. Turn left through two gates, and then turn right up a stone track signposted 'Sandy Gate', passing extensive limestone pavement on the left.

2. This track is called **Bycliffe Road** and where it turns sharp right (signposted 'Middlesmoor'), turn left through a gate signposted 'Capplestone Gate'.

*You are now on the '**Conistone Turf Road'**, used in bygone times to transport peat off the fells to heat cottages in the village. It was also a route for lead miners from Conistone Moorhead Mining*

Company until the mines closed in 1872.

The path follows a wall line and, at a small **plantation**, turns right up a **broad grassy track**, climbing to the left side of a limestone scar. Keep ahead aiming for the trig point at **Capplestone Gate** (512m/1680ft), the highest point of the walk.

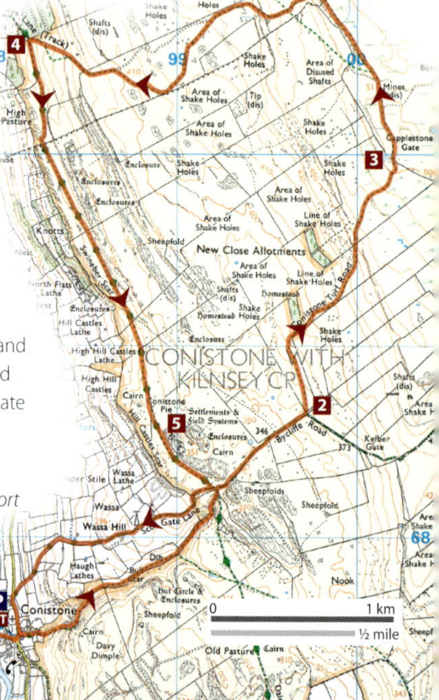

Scree on the flanks of Conistone Dib

Enjoy the extensive views over Great Whernside and Buckden Pike to the north, Malham Moor and Fountains Fell to the west and, in the far distance, Pendle Hill.

3. Cross the wall to the right of the trig point, signposted 'Kettlewell'. The boulder-strewn path, indistinct in places but with yellow markers, generally follows the wall line on the left, passing spoil tips from old lead mining activity. Ignore the first ladder stile on the left signposted 'Kettlewell', and keep ahead to reach a fence stile. Fifty metres later, turn left, downhill, over a ladder stile (no signpost).

Before descending, take a **detour** on a faint path following the wall on the right, to visit **Langcliffe Pot,** an enormous shake hole, from which emanates the sound of flowing water. *Do NOT go near the edge. It is a 90 ft pitch to enter what is considered by cavers to be one of the most dangerous caves in Britain.*

Return to the path and turn downhill. The path goes through a broken wall to enter a long field. Keep close to the wall on the right to reach a gate 50 metres before the wall corner. Turn right through the gate

Old Cote Moor and Littondale from Conistone Pie

onto a broad track heading north-west downhill to a gate into a **wood** where the path rejoins **The Dales Way**.

4. Do not go through the gate, but turn left, southwards, onto the Dales Way, initially following a wall on the right. For the next 2 kilometre the path links up a series of wall stiles on a level **limestone terrace**, passing extensive **limestone outcrops** and scree, with the valley on the right. This is **Swineber Scar**.

About 1½ kilometres further along the scar, take a short **detour** to the right to scramble up **Conistone Pie**.

Conistone Pie provides superb views over Wharfedale and of the side valley of Littondale. Across the valley is Kilnsey Crag, a truncated spur with a famous overhang formed by glacial action. The flat fields below the crag are a former glacial lake. Kilnsey had a monastic grange belonging to Fountains Abbey. Sheep were driven here from Malham Moor along Mastiles Lane to be sheared. Kilnsey was a key part of the network of packhorse routes linking Fountains Abbey and it's landholdings in the Dales. A manorial court may also have operated at Kilnsey.

5. Return to the Dales Way and some 400 metres later turn right downhill on a broad track called **Scot Gate Lane** soon passing a mobile phone mast.

As you descend, notice the medieval terracing or 'strip lynchets' fossilised in the last two fields on the left before you meet the road (see below). Turn left along the road into Conistone, passing the picturesque parish church, to complete the walk. ♦

Strip lynchets

The sloping fields to the north and south of Conistone provide some excellent examples of 'strip lynchets'. These medieval terraces were formed by ploughing across the slope and piling stones at the field edge, thus increasing the depth of soil, making them flatter and easier to cultivate. Some other fine local examples can be seen in the fields nearby between Linton and Thorpe.

Semerwater in sombre mood

Semerwater

A circular walk around one of only two upland lakes in the Yorkshire Dales

Distance/Time: 5½ miles/ 9 kilometres. Allow 3½ - 4 hrs

Start: Car park (fee), north end of Semerwater, Raydale DL8 3DJ

Grid ref: SD 922 876

Ordnance Survey Map: Explorer OL30 Yorkshire Dales Northern & Central areas, *Wensleydale & Swaledale*

After the Walk: Rose and Crown, Bainbridge DL8 3EE | 01969 650225 OR Corn Mill Tea Room, The Newkin, Bainbridge DL8 3EH | 01969 650212

Walk outline: This walk provides a grand clockwise circumnavigation of Semerwater visiting one of the hamlets in quiet Raydale. The route follows the eastern shore, visiting an ancient church, before arriving at lovely water meadows at the headwaters of the lake. The onward path to Marsett crosses Cragdale and Raydale becks, two of the main inflows into Semerwater. A sustained climb up to Carlows (500m/1640ft) is rewarded by superb views over Semerwater with Wensleydale beyond. A gentle descent across fields to the lakeside completes the walk.

Wensleydale sheep

Semerwater

Semerwater is one of only two natural lakes in the Yorkshire Dales, the other being Malham Tarn. It is an upland lime-rich glacial lake with an inflow from mountain streams; and an important wetland and meadow habitat deserving its status as a Site of Special Scientific Interest. The car park stands on a terminal moraine that dams the lake and includes distinctive boulders, known as The Carlow Stone and the Mermaid Stones. These are formed of Shap granite originating in what is now The Lake District, and deposited here by retreating glaciers during the last Ice Age.

Yellow flag iris

The Walk

1. Leaving the **car park** and with your back to the lake, turn right and walk up the road towards **Low Blean Farm**, home of 'Semerwater Watersports'. Opposite the farm, turn right onto a footpath signposted 'Stalling Busk 1¼ miles'. The path initially follows the **lake shore**, and then, gently climbing, enters **Semerwater Nature Reserve** (run by the Yorkshire Wildlife Trust).

A range of habitats including fen, marsh, hay meadows, and willow carr make up this Reserve at the south-west end of the lake with Marsett Meadows further upstream.

About 750 metres further on, the path passes a **ruined chapel** in a field to the right.

A stile provides access to this remote chapel, *once serving Raydale and the villages of Stalling Busk and Marsett. Built in 1722, it fell into disuse in 1909 when a more convenient church, St Matthews, was built in the Arts and Crafts style in the centre of Stalling Busk.*

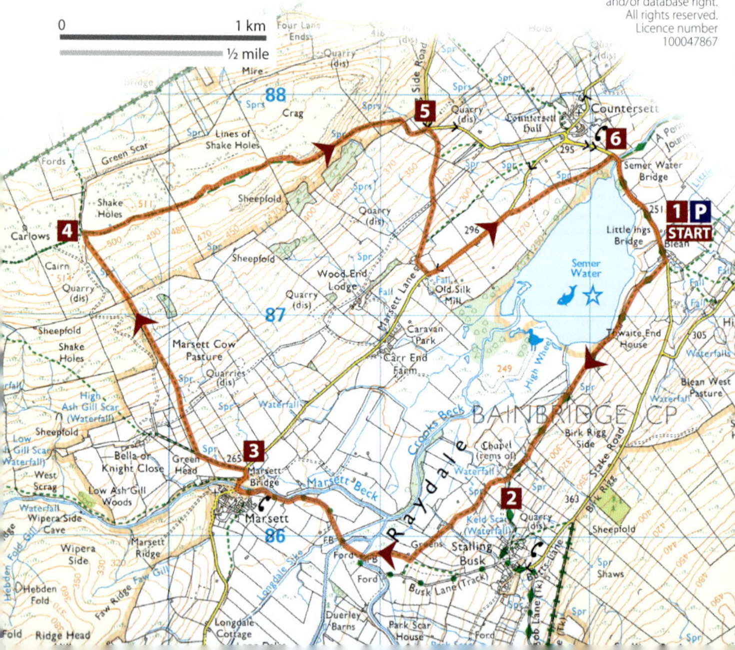

A Semerwater sunset

2. Return to the path and, in the next field, take the right-hand fork signposted 'Marsett'. Follow this path across five fields for about 500 metres and just after a field gate next to a barn, turn right, downhill, to follow the wall-line and cross a **footbridge** over **Cragdale Water** into delightful **water meadows.** Keep ahead to cross another **bridge** over **Raydale Beck**, and continue on a broad track following **Marsett Beck** into the village of **Marsett**.

3. At the end of the **village green**, turn right over the **road bridge**. Ignore the first path to the left and after 50 metres, turn left onto a farm track signposted 'Burtersett 2 miles, Hawes 3 miles'. After about 200 metres turn right through a gate (yellow marker) onto a footpath which follows a wall on the left for a sustained climb up the **fellside** for about 1 kilometre. Cross a ladder stile for the final 250 metres on open fell, aiming to the left of a **rocky outcrop** to arrive at a cross track and marker post. At 500 metres, this is the highest point of the walk.

The views over Semerwater, with Addlebrough (477m/1564ft) beyond, are

tremendous. To the west are the peaks of Wether Fell (614m/2014ft) and Yorburgh (515m/1690ft) with Wensleydale beyond.

Just below these two peaks, there is a Roman Road, known as Cam High Road, between Ingleton and the Roman fort at Bainbridge in Wensleydale. Until it was redirected through Hawes in 1795, this was also part of the Turnpike road between Richmond and Lancaster.

4. Turn right, north-eastwards, across the moor on a level track for about 1 kilometre to a slit-stile by a gate. The path bears right and begins to descend below some **craggy outcrops** and above woodland to reach a gate. Bear right on a track to reach a road.

5. From the road, immediately turn right over a ladder stile signposted 'Marsett Lane'. The way ahead descends diagonally across rough pasture, passing a lone tree to reach a gate near **farm buildings**. Bear left downhill on a farm track to reach **Marsett Lane**. Turn left on Marsett Lane and, after about 400 metres, turn right over a wall stile (signposted) and descend diagonally across meadows and then through scattered woodland to reach a road.

6. Turn right to cross **Semer Water Bridge** over the outflow from the lake to reach the **car park** at the end of the walk.

This outflow is the source of the River Bain,

a tributary of the River Ure and, at just 2¾ miles/4km, is one of the shortest named rivers in England. Semerwater is a glacial lake and the car park is on the glacial moraine damming the lake. The boulders around the water's edge are Shap Granite, evidence of the power of glaciers in moving rocks over large distances. ◆

Legend of the lake

In 'The Ballad of Semerwater', William Watson (1858-1935) wrote of 'a lost city in Semerwater, deep asleep till doom', a legend which may be linked to evidence of a prehistoric lake settlement. In 1937, a Bronze Age spearhead, now in the Dales Museum in Hawes, was found in Semerwater – probably placed there as a votive offering. The lake is likely to have had ritual significance in prehistoric times as a liminal space between this world and the next.

Cobbled street in Dent

Dentdale & Deepdale

Exhilarating walking on open moorland returning along the tree-lined riverside

Distance/Time: 5½ miles/9 kiloemtres. Allow 3½ - 4 hours

Start: Dent village car park

Grid ref: SD 704 870

Ordnance Survey Map: Explorer OL2 Yorkshire Dales Southern & Western Areas, *Whernside, Ingleborough & Pen-y-ghent*

After the Walk: Stone Close Tea Room, Main St, Dent, LA10 5QL | 015396 25231 | www.stonehouse.com OR The George and Dragon, Main St, Dent, LA10 5QL | 015396 25256

Walk outline: Leaving Dent village, the route follows the deeply-incised Flinter Gill, which drains the northern slope of Great Coum high above Dent. On reaching moorland, the way continues on a contouring path providing great views over heavily-wooded Dentdale with Whernside ahead, before descending into quiet Deepdale to follow the beck down to meet the River Dee in the valley bottom. From here it is an easy riverside stroll following the Dales Way to reach Church Bridge and a short walk into Dent.

Victorian postbox

Dentdale and Deepdale

Wainwright said 'Dent is not of this world…it's a place of cobbles, of jutting gables, overhanging roofs, quaint alleys, wooden galleries and outside staircases.' The village nestles in one of the most picturesque dales with flower-filled meadows and lush riverside pastures. The River Dee, a tributary of the River Lune, is one of the few Dales' rivers to drain westwards into the Irish Sea. The micro-brewery at Cowgill is the remotest in England, and Dent Station is equally remote — all of 4½ miles from Dent. The quiet side-dale of Deepdale bisects the looming bulks of Whernside (736m/2419ft) and Great Coum 687m/2250ft).

Peacock butterfly

The Walk

1. Leaving the **car park**, cross the road and walk up the lane to the left of the **Village Hall**. Where the road swings to the left, keep ahead signposted 'Flinter Gill'. A narrow stony path into **woodland** soon widens onto an **ancient track** ascending the fell with the deeply-incised **Flinter Gill** on the left.

Keep ahead passing the '**wishing tree**' and an old **lime kiln** until the track enters **moorland**. After 200 metres, the track arrives at a T-junction with **Green Lane**.

Formerly a packhorse route between Barbon and Ingleton, this track is known locally as 'Occupation Road'. The name dates back to the Enclosure Acts of the 1850s as it served the farmers, who were responsible for enclosing or 'occupying' the moorland, by dividing the land into large allotments for grazing – regarded by locals as theft on a grand scale. The imposing whaleback hill to the west is Middleton Fell.

2. Turn left, south-eastwards, signposted 'High Moss 4 miles'. Continue on Green Lane for about 2 kilometres, enjoying superb views to the left over the upper part of Dentdale and the Pennine watershed, with the imposing bulk of Whernside (736m) ahead. At a

T-junction, turn left downhill signposted 'Nun House Outrake'.

Eventually, this stony track reaches a road (**Deepdale Lane**). Cross the road signposted 'Mill Bridge ½ mile'. Pass through two gates and then bear right through another gate into a narrow field which descends to an abandoned farmhouse called **Scow**.

3. Pass between the farmhouse and the barn and turn left into a wide field with a yellow waymarker ahead.

Green Lane above Dentdale – view of the Howgills

Continue across three fields, keeping well above the woodland on the right which surrounds Deepdale Beck, to reach the road at **Mill Bridge**. Do not cross the bridge, but turn left and then immediately right signposted 'Church Bridge 1 mile'.

4. The path follows **Deepdale Beck** to it's confluence with the **River Dee** and then continues for 1½ kilometres towards **Church Bridge**. Just before the bridge the path leaves the river, turning left across fields, before turning right to meet the road just above Church Bridge.

5. Turn left up the road into the **village** and turn right through the **churchyard** to complete the walk. ◆

The 'terrible knitters' of Dent

To supplement poor wages from farming and lead-mining, villagers took up knitting. Such was the extraordinary speed and quality of their work, that they earned the reputation of 'terrible' (meaning 'awe-inspiring') knitters. To save on fuel and light, villagers would meet in the evening at one cottage to tell stories and sing songs as they knitted. Trade peaked during the Napoleonic Wars when the army needed knitted socks.

Useful Information

'Welcome to Yorkshire'
Yorkshire's official website covers everything from accommodation, events, attractions, and festivals: www.yorkshire.com

Yorkshire Dales National Park
The National Park website also has information on what to see and do. See the webpage 'Visit the Dales' in particular at **www.yorkshiredales.org.uk**. There are YDNP Visitor Centres at Aysgarth, Grassington, Hawes, Malham and Reeth.

Tourist Information Centres

Appleby	017683 51177	tic@applebytown.org.uk
Settle	01729 825192	settle@ytbtic.co.uk
Grassington	01756 751 690	grassington@yorkshiredales.org.uk
Ingleton	015242 41701	ingletontic@btconnect.com
Hawes	01969 666 210	hawes@yorkshiredales.org.uk
Leyburn	01969 623814	www.welcometoleyburn.co.uk
Sedbergh	01539 620125	tic@sedbergh.org.uk
Malham	01729 833200	malham@yorkshiredales.org.uk
Skipton	01756 792809	skiptontic@cravendc.gov.uk

Local Museums

Dales Countryside Museum, Station Yard, Burtersett Road, Hawes, DL8 3NT
The Dales largest and arguably best museum. Fascinating archaeology, history, wildlife, and geology. **www.dalescountrysidemuseum.org.uk** | 01969 666210 | dcm@yorkshiredales.org.uk

le Museum, The Green, Reeth, Richmond DL11 6TX
Covers rural history of life and work in Swaledale and Arkengarthdale.
www.swaledalemuseum.org.uk | 01748 884118 | museum.swaledale@btinternet.com

Grassington Folk Museum, Main Street, Grassington, Skipton BD23 5AQ
Covers period costumes, folklore, lead mining, Dales farming | 01756 753287 | uwmsoc@gmail.com

Museum of North Craven Life, The Folly, Victoria St, Settle BD24 9EY
Reflects the social, cultural, and industrial heritage of North Craven.
www.thefolly.org.uk | 01729 825185

Weather
Five day forecast for The Yorkshire Dales: 0300 456 0030
www.yorkshiredales.org.uk/visit-the-dales/essential-information/weather